Informing the legislative debate since 1914

Iran: U.S. Economic Sanctions and the Authority to Lift Restrictions

Dianne E. Rennack

Specialist in Foreign Policy Legislation

November 15, 2013

Congressional Research Service

7-5700

www.crs.gov

R43311

Summary

The United States has led the international community in imposing economic sanctions on Iran, in an effort to change the government of that country's support of acts of international terrorism, poor human rights record, weapons and missile development and acquisition, role in regional instability, and development of a nuclear program.

This report identifies the legislative bases for sanctions imposed on Iran, and the nature of the authority to waive or lift those restrictions. It comprises two tables that present legislation and executive orders that are specific to Iran and its objectionable activities in the areas of terrorism, human rights, and weapons proliferation. It will be updated if and when new legislation is enacted, or, in the case of executive orders, if and when the President takes additional steps to change U.S. policy toward Iran.

Other CRS reports address the U.S.-Iran relationship, including a comprehensive discussion of the practical application of economic sanctions: CRS Report RS20871, *Iran Sanctions*, by Kenneth Katzman. See also CRS Report RL32048, *Iran: U.S. Concerns and Policy Responses*, by Kenneth Katzman, and CRS Report R40094, *Iran's Nuclear Program: Tehran's Compliance with International Obligations*, by Paul K. Kerr.

Contents

Tables

Contacts

Overview

The regime of economic sanctions against Iran is arguably the most complex the United States and the international community have ever imposed on a rogue state. Iran's economy was once integrated into world trade, markets, and banking. As relations deteriorated, for the United States starting during Iran's 1979 revolution and hostage-taking at the U.S. Embassy, and for the larger international community over more recent human rights and nuclear proliferation concerns, this complete economic integration offered seemingly limitless opportunities to impose economic restrictions and create points where pressure could be applied to bring Iran back into conformity with international norms.

The June 2013 election of President Hassan Rouhani seems to have created the possibility of an opening between the United States and Iran. The presidents of each nation addressed a fall meeting of the U.N. General Assembly, and spoke directly to one another shortly thereafter—the first direct contact at the top level in 34 years. Diplomatic staff representing the United States, Russia, China, France, Britain (permanent members of the U.N. Security Council), plus Germany (P5+1), met with Iran's foreign ministry in mid-October 2013 on the heels of that contact. Over November 7-9, 2013, these negotiators drafted an interim deal that would require Iran to limit its nuclear program and, in exchange, require the United States and others to ease economic sanctions affecting Iran's access to some of its hard currency held abroad. The P5+1 and Iran negotiators are expected to meet again in late November 2013.

The sudden possibility that the United States may ease financial sector sanctions, and perhaps commit to an eventual dismantling of the entire panoply of economic restrictions on Iran affecting aid, trade, shipping, banking, insurance, underwriting, and support in the international financial institutions, arrives at a time when Congress has been considering additional sanctions on Iran. The House adopted H.R. 850, the Nuclear Iran Prevention Act of 2013, on July 31, 2013, by a vote of 400-20. That act would require new economic restrictions on trade in cars manufacturing and extractive industries, further impede financial activities, and place greater demands for sanctions compliance by third countries. In the Senate, H.R. 850 was referred to the Committee on Banking, Housing, and Urban Affairs. Other pending legislative proposals, most notably the National Defense Authorization Act for Fiscal Year 2014 (S. 1197; H.R. 1960),[1] could provide immediate means for Congress to influence the United States' approach to any negotiations going forward.

Authority to Waive or Lift Economic Sanctions

The ability to impose and ease economic sanctions with some nimbleness and responsiveness to changing events is key to effectively using the tool in furtherance of national security or foreign policy objectives. Historically, both the President and Congress have recognized this essential requirement and have worked together to provide the President substantial flexibility. In the collection of laws that are the statutory basis for the U.S. economic sanctions regime on Iran, the President retains, in varying degrees, the authority to tighten and relax restrictions.

---

[1] National defense authorization acts were used to enact new sanctions and amend existing provisions on Iran in FY2010, FY2012, and FY2013.

In the Comprehensive Iran Sanctions, Accountability, and Divestment Act of 2010 (CISADA; P.L. 111-195, as amended; 22 U.S.C. 8501 *et seq.*),[2] Congress grants to the President the authority to terminate most of the sanctions imposed on Iran in that act as well as the Iran Threat Reduction and Syria Human Rights Act of 2012 (P.L. 112-158; 22 U.S.C. 8701 *et seq.*), and Iran Freedom and Counter-proliferation Act of 2012 (P.L. 112-239; 22 U.S.C. 8801 *et seq.*). Before terminating these sanctions, however, the President must certify that the government of Iran has ceased its engagement in the two critical areas of terrorism and weapons, as set forth in Section 401 of CISADA—

> SEC. 401 [22 U.S.C. 8551]. GENERAL PROVISIONS.
>
> (a) SUNSET.—The provisions of this Act (other than sections 105 and 305 and the amendments made by sections 102, 107, 109, and 205) shall terminate, and section 13(c)(1)(B) of the Investment Company Act of 1940, as added by section 203(a), shall cease to be effective, on the date that is 30 days after the date on which the President certifies to Congress that—
>
> > (1) the Government of Iran has ceased providing support for acts of international terrorism and no longer satisfies the requirements for designation as a state sponsor of terrorism (as defined in section 301) under—
> >
> > > (A) section 6(j)(1)(A) of the Export Administration Act of 1979 (50 U.S.C. App. 2405(j)(1)(A)) (or any successor thereto);
> > >
> > > (B) section 40(d) of the Arms Export Control Act (22 U.S.C. 2780(d)); or
> > >
> > > (C) section 620A(a) of the Foreign Assistance Act of 1961 (22 U.S.C. 2371(a)); and
> >
> > (2) Iran has ceased the pursuit, acquisition, and development of, and verifiably dismantled its, nuclear, biological, and chemical weapons and ballistic missiles and ballistic missile launch technology.
>
> (b) PRESIDENTIAL WAIVERS.—
>
> > (1) IN GENERAL.—The President may waive the application of sanctions under section 103(b), the requirement to impose or maintain sanctions with respect to a person under section 105(a), 105A(a), 105B(a), or 105C(a) the requirement to include a person on the list required by section 105(b), 105A(b), 105B(b), or 105C(b), the application of the prohibition under section 106(a), or the imposition of the licensing requirement under section 303(c) with respect to a country designated as a Destination of Diversion Concern under section 303(a), if the President determines that such a waiver is in the national interest of the United States.

---

[2] Section 401(a) and (b)(1) of the Comprehensive Iran Sanctions, Accountability, and Divestment Act of 2010 (CISADA; P.L. 111-195; 22 U.S.C. 8551), as amended. **Table 1** shows the sanctions for which Section 401 waiver authority is applicable.

International Terrorism Determination

To lift the majority of the economic sanctions imposed by CISADA, the President must determine and certify that the government of Iran no longer supports acts of international terrorism. The government of Iran is designated as a state sponsor of acts of international terrorism, effective January 1984, pursuant to the Secretary of State's authorities and responsibilities under Section 6(j) of the Export Administration Act of 1979. Various statutes impede or prohibit foreign aid, financing, and trade because of that designation. Three laws (§620A, Foreign Assistance Act of 1961 [22 U.S.C. 2371]; §40, Arms Export Control Act [22 U.S.C. 2780]; and §6(j), Export Administration Act of 1979 [50 U.S.C. app. 2405(j)]) form the "terrorist list."[3] Because these statutes are not Iran-specific, they are not included in **Table 1**.

The President holds the authority to remove the designation of any country from the terrorist list. Though each of the three laws provides slightly different procedures, the authority to delist Iran resides with the President, and generally requires him to find that

- there has been a fundamental change in the leadership and policies of the government;

- the government is not supporting acts of international terrorism; and

- the government has assured that it will not support terrorism in the future.

Alternatively, the President may notify Congress that the terrorism designation will be rescinded in 45 days, and that the rescission is justified on the basis that

- the government has not supported an act of terrorism in the preceding six months; and

- the government has assured that it will not support terrorism in the future.

In the case of foreign aid, the President also is authorized to provide aid despite the terrorism designation if he finds that "national security interests or humanitarian reasons justify" doing so and so notifies Congress 15 days in advance. In practical terms, the process of removing a state from the list of sponsors of international terrorism is studied and argued throughout the entire executive branch interagency, with those departments that are tasked with administering the restrictions—primarily State, Commerce, Treasury, Justice, and Defense—each weighing in. For a state to be delisted—which has occurred, most recently, to North Korea and Libya—the Secretary of State publishes a public notice that the respective government no longer supports acts of international terrorism; that starts the six-month countdown required by legislation. After six months (or later), both the President and the Secretary of State issue determinations and announcements, which is followed by a rewriting of each department's regulations governing exports, arms sales, transactions, and other related matters.

---

[3] §40A, Arms Export Control Act (22 U.S.C. 2780) also prohibits trade in defense articles and defense services to any country the President finds "is not cooperating fully with Untied States antiterrorism efforts." The President may waive the prohibition if he finds it "important to the national interests" to do so. This provision requires the President to annually identify uncooperative states; Iran has been listed since the provision's enactment in 1996 (first list was issued in 1997; authority to make certifications is currently delegated to the Secretary of State).

Legislation and Executive Orders

The two tables presented in this report identify the legislative bases for sanctions imposed on Iran, and the nature of the authority to waive or lift those restrictions. **Table 1** presents legislation, and **Table 2** shows executive orders that are specific to Iran and its objectionable activities in the areas of terrorism, human rights, and weapons proliferation.

Public laws that are not specific to the objectionable activities of the government of Iran but have been invoked to impede transactions or other economic or diplomatic relations are not included here. Failure to achieve human rights standards as a condition for foreign aid (e.g., the Foreign Assistance Act of 1961, the Trafficking Victims Protection Act of 2000, and related annual appropriations), or refusal to comply with international nonproliferation norms (e.g., Chemical and Biological Weapons Control and Warfare Elimination Act of 1991), for example, can trigger a range of economic sanctions. These and other authorities have been applied to Iran. It is unlikely that these statutes would be amended if and when they no longer apply to Iran. Sanctions authorized by these statutes are applied, and lifted, by executive branch decision.

On the other hand, because the President holds sole authority to renew, alter, and revoke executive orders he issues pursuant to the National Emergencies Act (NEA) and the International Emergency Economic Powers Act (IEEPA), **Table 2** includes actions taken that are specific to Iran and also actions taken that are not specific to Iran (e.g., Executive Order 13224 and 13382 target terrorists and proliferators, respectively) but have been applied to that country. The authorities in these orders have been exercised to affect Iran in a significant way. Executive orders are subject to their underlying statutory authorities: economic sanctions are most often based on the President's authorities established in IEEPA. These are applied and lifted by the President; often their implementation and administration are delegated to the Secretary of the Treasury, who in turn assigns the task to Treasury's Office of Foreign Assets Control. Many of the Iran-specific sanctions in statute cite the President's authority to curtail transactions under IEEPA. In some instances, Congress has enacted restrictions on the President's unilateral authority to revoke an order, and the economic restrictions therein, until specific conditions are met.

Table 1. Iran—Economic Sanctions Currently Imposed in Furtherance of U.S. Foreign Policy or National Security Objectives

Statutory Basis	Rationale	Restriction	Authority To Impose	Authority To Lift or Waive
FOREIGN AID: AUTHORIZATION AND APPROPRIATIONS				
Sec. 307, **Foreign Assistance Act of 1961** (P.L. 87-195; 22 U.S.C. 2227; as amended)	General foreign policy reasons	Limits proportionate share of foreign aid to international organizations which, in turn, expend funds in Iran.	Statutory requirement	No waiver; exemption for certain UNICEF and IAEA programs. Secretary of State may block funds if he determines that IAEA programs are "inconsistent with U.S. nonproliferation and safety goals, will provide Iran with training or expertise ..., or are being used as a cover for the acquisition of sensitive nuclear technology" and notifies Congress.
Sec. 7007, **Foreign Operations Appropriations** (P.L. 112-74; 125 Stat. 1195; as continued)	General foreign policy reasons	Prohibits direct funding to the Government of Iran, including Export-Import Bank funds.	Statutory requirement	No waiver, though "notwithstanding" clauses elsewhere in appropriations and authorization statutes could result in aid being made available.
Sec. 7015(f), **Foreign Operations Appropriations** (P.L. 112-74; 125 Stat. 1195; as continued)	General foreign policy reasons	Prohibits most foreign aid to Iran, "except as provided through the regular notification procedures of the Committees on Appropriations."	Statutory requirement	President may waive or lift by exercising notification procedures of the Committee on Appropriations.
Sec. 7041(c), **Foreign Operations Appropriations** (P.L. 112-74; 125 Stat. 1224; as continued)	Nuclear nonproliferation	Prohibits U.S. Export-Import Bank from providing financing "to any person that is subject to sanctions under" Sec. 5(a)(2) or (3) of the Iran Sanctions Act of 1996—those under sanctions for engaging in production or export to Iran of refined petroleum products.	Statutory requirement	No waiver, though those sanctioned under Sec. 5(a)(2) and (3), Iran Sanctions Act of 1996, is subject to change. See below.
Sec. 7070(b)(1)(A), **Foreign Operations Appropriations**	Nuclear and missile nonproliferation	Withholds 60% of funds intended for **Russia** under "Assistance for Europe, Eurasia and Central Asia."	Statutory requirement	President determines and certifies to Committees on Appropriations that Russia "has terminated implementation of arrangements to provide Iran with technical

Statutory Basis	Rationale	Restriction	Authority To Impose	Authority To Lift or Waive
(P.L. 112-74; 125 Stat. 1254; as continued)				expertise, training, technology, or equipment necessary to develop a nuclear reactor, related nuclear research facilities or programs, or ballistic missile capability."

IRAQ SANCTIONS ACT OF 1990

(P.L. 101-513; 50 U.S.C. 1701 note; extended to apply to Iran by Sec. 1603 of the Iran-Iraq Arms Non-proliferation Act of 1992; see below)

Statutory Basis	Rationale	Restriction	Authority To Impose	Authority To Lift or Waive
Sec. 586G	Nonproliferation	Prohibits: —Sales under the Arms Export Control Act (foreign military sales); —Export licenses for commercial arms sales for any USML item; —Export of Commerce Control List items; and —export of nuclear equipment, materials, or technology.	Statutory requirement	President may waive if he finds it "essential to the national interest" to do so and notifies the Armed Services, Foreign Affairs/Relations Committees 15 days in advance (Sec. 1606, IIANA).

IRAN-IRAQ ARMS NON-PROLIFERATION ACT OF 1992 (IIANA)

(Title XVI of P.L. 102-484 (National Defense Authorization Act for Fiscal Year 1993); 50 U.S.C. 1701 note; as amended)

Statutory Basis	Rationale	Restriction	Authority To Impose	Authority To Lift or Waive
Sec. 1603	Nonproliferation	Makes selected sanctions in Sec. 586G, Iran Sanctions Act of 1990, applicable for Iran (see above).		President may waive; see Sec. 586G, Iran Sanctions Act of 1990, above.
Sec. 1604	Nonproliferation	For a period of 2 years, for any **person** who "transfers goods or technology so as to contribute knowingly and materially" to Iran's efforts "to acquire chemical, biological, or nuclear weapons or to acquire destabilizing numbers and types of advanced conventional weapons": —prohibits USG procurement contracts; and —prohibits U.S. export licenses.	Statutory requirement	President may waive if he finds it "essential to the national interest" to do so and notifies the Armed Services, Foreign Affairs/Relations Committees 15 days in advance (Sec. 1606, IIANA).
Sec. 1605	Nonproliferation	For any **foreign government** that "transfers or retransfers goods or technology so as to	Statutory requirement	President may waive if he finds it "essential to the national interest" to do so and notifies

Statutory Basis	Rationale	Restriction	Authority To Impose	Authority To Lift or Waive
		contribute knowingly and materially" to Iran's efforts "to acquire chemical, biological, or nuclear weapons or to acquire destabilizing numbers and types of advanced conventional weapons": —Suspends foreign aid for one year; —Requires US opposition and "no" votes in international financial institutions for one year; —Suspends weapons codevelopment and coproduction agreements for one year; —Suspends exchange agreements and related exports pertaining to military and dual-use technology for one year (unless such activities contribute to US security); and —Prohibits the export of USML items for one year.		the Armed Services, Foreign Affairs/Relations Committees 15 days in advance (Sec. 1606, IIANA).
Sec. 1605(c)	Nonproliferation	The President may exercise IEEPA authorities, excluding instances of "urgent humanitarian assistance," toward the foreign country. (See IEEPA authorities, below.)	At the President's discretion	At the President's discretion, following IEEPA authorities (see below).

IRAN SANCTIONS ACT OF 1996 (ISA 1996)

(P.L. 104-172; 50 U.S.C. 1701 note; as amended; Act sunsets effective December 31, 2016 (Sec. 13(b)))

Statutory Basis	Rationale	Restriction	Authority To Impose	Authority To Lift or Waive
Sec. 5(a), Sec, 6	Nonproliferation Anti-terrorism	Sec. 5(a) identifies developing Iran's energy sector as behavior to be investigated and cause for sanctions: —investing in Iran's petroleum resources; —providing to Iran goods, services, technology, information, or support relating to production of refined petroleum products; —trades in, facilitates, or finances Iran's refined petroleum products;	President imposes, based on investigation (Sec. 4(e)). Generally, imposed for a period of 2 years (Sec. 9(b)). President may delay imposition of sanctions for up to 90 days in order to initiate consultations with foreign government of jurisdiction (Sec. 9(a)).	The President may waive, case-by-case, for 6 months and for further 6-12 months depending on circumstances, for a foreign national if he finds it "vital to the national security interests" and notifies the Committees on Finance, Banking, Foreign Relations. Foreign Affairs, Ways and Means, Financial Services, 30 days in advance (Sec. 4(c)). The President may waive for 12 months if the targeted person is subject to a government

Statutory Basis	Rationale	Restriction	Authority To Impose	Authority To Lift or Waive
		—joint ventures with the Government of Iran to develop refined petroleum resources;		cooperating with U.S. in multilateral nonproliferation efforts relating to Iran, it is vital to national security interests, and he notifies Congress 30 days in advance.
		—supporting Iran's development of petroleum products;		The President may cancel an investigation (precursor to imposing sanctions) if he determines the person is no longer engaged in objectionable behavior and has credible assurances such behavior will not occur in the future (Sec. 4(e)).
		—supporting Iran's development of petrochemical products;		The President may not apply sanctions if transaction:
		—transporting crude oil from Iran; and		—meets an existing contract requirement;
		—concealing Iran origin of petroleum products in the course of transporting such products.		—is completed by a sole source supplier; or
		President may choose among the following penalties, and is required to impose at least five (Sec. 6):		—is "essential to the national security under defense coproduction agreements";
		—deny Export-Import Bank program funds;		—is specifically designated under certain trade laws;
		—deny export licenses;		—complies with existing contracts and pertains to spare parts, component parts, servicing and maintenance, or information and technology relating to essential U.S. products, or medicine, medical supplies or humanitarian items (Sec. 6(f)).
		—prohibit loans from U.S. financial institutions;		The requirement to impose sanctions under Sec. 5(a) has no force or effect if the President determines Iran:
		—prohibit targeted financial institutions being designated as a primary dealer or a repository of government funds;		—has ceased programs relating to nuclear weapons, chemical and biological weapons, ballistic missiles;
		—deny U.S. government procurement contracts;		—is no longer designated as a state supporter of acts of international terrorism; and
		—limit or prohibit foreign exchange transactions;		—"poses no significant threat to United
		—limit or prohibit transactions with banks under U.S. jurisdiction;		
		—prohibit transactions related to U.S.-based property;		
		—prohibit investments in equity of a targeted entity;		
		—deny visas to, or expel, any person who holds a position or controlling interest in a targeted		

Statutory Basis	Rationale	Restriction	Authority To Impose	Authority To Lift or Waive
		entity; —impose any of the above on a targeted entity's principal executive officers; and —economic restrictions drawing from IEEPA authorities (see below).		States national security, interests, or allies." (Sec. 8). President may lift sanctions if he determines behavior has changed (Sec. 9(b)(2)). President may waive sanctions if he determines it is "essential to national security interests" to do so (Sec. 9(c)). President may delay imposition of sanctions expanded by amendments in the Comprehensive Iran Sanctions, Accountability, and Divestment Act (CISADA), relating to development and export of refined petroleum products, for up to 180 days, and in additional 180-day increments, if President certifies objectionable activities are being curtailed (CISADA, Sec. 102(h)). President may waive contractor certification requirement, case-by-case, if he finds it "essential to national security interests" to do so (Sec. 6(b)(5)).
Sec. 5(b), Sec. 6	Nonproliferation Anti-terrorism	All US government agencies are required to certify any prospective contractor as not being subject to sanctions under this section (Sec. 6(b)). Sec. 5(b) identifies developing Iran's WMD or other military capabilities as cause for sanctions: —exports, transfers, and transshipments of military/weapons goods, services, or technology; and —joint ventures relating to uranium mining, production, or transportation. President may choose among the following penalties, and is required to impose at least five (Sec. 6): —deny Export-Import Bank program funds; —deny export licenses;	Statutory requirement; generally imposed for a period of 2 years (Sec. 9(b)). President may delay imposition of sanctions for up to 90 days in order to initiate consultations with foreign government of jurisdiction (Sec. 9(a)).	The President may not apply sanctions if: —in the case of joint venture, is terminated within 180 days; —President determines the government of jurisdiction did not know person was engaged in activity, or has taken steps to prevent recurrence; —case-by-case, President determines approval of activity is "vital to national security interests of the United States" and notifies Congress; or The President may not apply sanctions if

Statutory Basis	Rationale	Restriction	Authority To Impose	Authority To Lift or Waive
		—prohibit loans from U.S. financial institutions;		transaction:
		—prohibit targeted financial institutions being designated as a primary dealer or a repository of government funds;		—meets an existing contract requirement;
				—is completed by a sole source supplier; or
		—deny U.S. government procurement contracts;		—is "essential to the national security under defense coproduction agreements";
		—limit or prohibit foreign exchange transactions;		—is specifically designated under certain trade laws;
		—limit or prohibit transactions with banks under U.S. jurisdiction;		—complies with existing contracts and pertains to spare parts, component parts, servicing and maintenance, or information and technology relating to essential US products, or medicine, medical supplies or humanitarian items (Sec. 5(f)).
		—prohibit transactions related to U.S.-based property;		
		—prohibit investments in equity of a targeted entity;		
		—deny visas to, or expel, any person who holds a position or controlling interest in a targeted entity;		
		—impose any of the above on a targeted entity's principal executive officers; and		President may waive contractor certification requirement, case-by-case, if he finds it "essential to national security interests" to do so (Sec. 6(b)(5)).
		—economic restrictions drawing from IEEPA authorities (see below).		President may lift sanctions if he determines behavior has changed (Sec. 9(b)(2)).
		All US government agencies are required to certify any prospective contractor as not being subject to sanctions under this section (Sec. 6(b)).		President may waive sanctions if he determines it is "essential to national security interests" to do so (Sec. 9(c)).

IRAN, NORTH KOREA, AND SYRIA NONPROLIFERATION ACT (INKSA)

(P.L. 106-178; 50 U.S.C. 1701 note; as amended)

Statutory Basis	Rationale	Restriction	Authority To Impose	Authority To Lift or Waive
Sec. 3	Nonproliferation	Foreign persons identified by President as having transferred to or acquired from Iran goods, services, or technology related to weapons or missile proliferation may, at the President's	At the President's discretion	President may choose to not impose sanctions, but must justify to Committees on Foreign Affairs and Foreign Relations (Sec. 4).

Statutory Basis	Rationale	Restriction	Authority To Impose	Authority To Lift or Waive
		discretion, be: —denied entering into procurement contracts with the US government; —prohibited transactions relating to import into the United States; —prohibited arms sales from the United States of USML articles and services; —denied export licenses for items controlled under the Export Administration Act of 1979 or Export Administration Regulations.		President may choose to not impose sanctions if he finds: —targeted person did not *knowingly* engage in objectionable transaction; —transaction did not *materially* contribute to proliferation; —government of jurisdiction adheres to relevant nonproliferation regime; or —government of jurisdiction "has imposed meaningful penalties" (Sec. 5(a)).

TRADE SANCTIONS REFORM AND EXPORT ENHANCEMENT ACT OF 2000 (TSRA)

(Title IX of P.L. 106-387 (Agriculture, Rural Development, Food and Drug Administration, and Related Agencies Appropriations Act, 2001); 22 U.S.C. 7201 et seq.; as amended)

Statutory Basis	Rationale	Restriction	Authority To Impose	Authority To Lift or Waive
Sec. 906 (22 U.S.C. 7205)	Anti-terrorism	Requires export licenses for agricultural commodities, medicines, medical devices to any government designated as a state sponsor of acts of international terrorism.	Statutory requirement	No waiver; the executive branch (primarily Departments of Commerce, for exportation, and Treasury for related transactions) may issue export licenses limited to a 12-month duration but there is no limit on the number or nature of licenses generally.
Sec. 908 (22 U.S.C. 7207)	Anti-terrorism	Prohibits U.S. assistance—foreign aid, export assistance, credits, guarantees—for commercial exports to Iran.	Statutory requirement	President may waive if "it is in the national security interest of the United States to do so, or for humanitarian reasons."

IRAN NUCLEAR PROLIFERATION PREVENTION ACT OF 2002 (INPPA)

(Subtitle D of title XIII of P.L. 107-228 (Foreign Relations Authorization Act for Fiscal Year 2003)

Statutory Basis	Rationale	Restriction	Authority To Impose	Authority To Lift or Waive
Sec. 1343(b) (22 U.S.C. 2027(b))	Nonproliferation	Requires the U.S. representative to the IAEA to oppose programs that are "inconsistent with nuclear nonproliferation and safety goals of the United States."	Discretionary, based on findings of the Secretary of State	No waiver; however, "nay" votes are based on the Secretary of State's annual review of IAEA programs and determinations.

Statutory Basis	Rationale	Restriction	Authority To Impose	Authority To Lift or Waive

IRAN FREEDOM SUPPORT ACT (IFSA)

(P.L. 109-293; 50 U.S.C. 1701 note)

Statutory Basis	Rationale	Restriction	Authority To Impose	Authority To Lift or Waive
Sec. 101	Democracy promotion General foreign policy reasons	Makes permanent the restrictions the President imposed under IEEPA/NEA authorities in Executive Order 12957, which: —prohibits any U.S. person from entering into a contract or financing or guaranteeing performance under a contract relating to petroleum resource development in Iran; and Executive Order 12959, which: —prohibits any U.S. person from investing in Iran; and Executive Order 13059, which: —prohibits any U.S. person from exporting where the end-user is Iran or the Government of Iran; —prohibits any U.S. person from investing in Iran; —prohibits any U.S. person from engaging in transactions or financing related to Iran-origin goods or services.	Statutory requirement	President may terminate the sanctions if he notifies Congress 15 days in advance, unless "exigent circumstances" warrant terminating the restrictions without notice, in which case Congress shall be notified within 3 days after termination.

COMPREHENSIVE IRAN SANCTIONS, ACCOUNTABILITY, AND DIVESTMENT ACT OF 2010 (CISADA)

(P.L. 111-195; 22 U.S.C. 8501 et seq.; as amended)

Statutory Basis	Rationale	Restriction	Authority To Impose	Authority To Lift or Waive
Sec. 103(b)(1) and (2) (22 U.S.C. 8512)	Nonproliferation Human rights Anti-terrorism	Prohibits most imports into the United States of goods of Iranian origin. Prohibits a U.S. person from exporting most U.S.-origin goods, services, or technology to Iran.	Statutory requirement	Allows imports, exports, food, medicine, and humanitarian aid as covered by IEEPA and TSRA. President may allow exports if he determines to do so is in the national interest. Most of CISADA, including sanctions under this section, ceases to be effective when

Statutory Basis	Rationale	Restriction	Authority To Impose	Authority To Lift or Waive
				President removes Iran's designation as a sponsor of acts of international terrorism and that country has ceased its pursuit of weapons of mass destruction (WMD) (Sec. 401; 22 U.S.C. 8551).
				President may waive if he finds it "in the national interest" to do so (Sec. 401(b)).
Sec. 103(b)(3) (22 U.S.C. 8512)	Nonproliferation Human rights Anti-terrorism	Freezes assets of individual, family member, or associates acting on behalf of individual, in compliance with IEEPA authorities.	President determines	President's discretion.
				Most of CISADA, including sanctions under this section, ceases to be effective when President removes Iran's designation as a sponsor of acts of international terrorism and that country has ceased its pursuit of WMD (Sec. 401; 22 U.S.C. 8551).
				President may waive if he finds it "in the national interest" to do so (Sec. 401(b)).
Sec. 104(c) (22 U.S.C. 8513(c))	Anti-money laundering Anti-terrorism (financing) Nonproliferation	Imposes IEEPA-authorized economic restrictions, to be issued by Secretary of the Treasury in new regulations and prohibits U.S. banks opening or maintaining correspondent or payable-through accounts for any foreign financial institution that: —facilitates Iran's acquisition of WMD; —facilitates Iran's support of foreign terrorist organizations (FTO); —facilitates activities of persons subject to U.N. Security Council sanctions; —engages in money laundering; —facilitates Iran's Central Bank or other financial institution in objectionable activities; or —facilitates transactions of IRGC or others under IEEPA sanctions.	Statutory requirement	Secretary of the Treasury may waive if he finds it "necessary to the national interest" to do so (subsec. (f)). Most of CISADA, including sanctions under this section, ceases to be effective when President removes Iran's designation as a sponsor of acts of international terrorism and that country has ceased its pursuit of WMD (Sec. 401; 22 U.S.C. 8551).

Statutory Basis	Rationale	Restriction	Authority To Impose	Authority To Lift or Waive
Sec. 104(c)(4) (22 U.S.C. 8513(c)(4))	Anti-money laundering Anti-terrorism (financing) Nonproliferation	Subjects National Iranian Oil Company (NIOC) and National Iranian Tanker Company (NITC) to IEEPA-authorized economic restrictions, promulgated by the Secretary of the Treasury under Sec. 104(c) (above) if found to be affiliated with the Iranian Revolutionary Guard Corps (IRGC).	Requires Secretary of the Treasury determination	Secretary of the Treasury may waive if he finds it "necessary to the national interest" to do so (subsec. (f)). If the country of primary jurisdiction is exempted under Sec. 1245, National Defense Authorization Act, 2012 (NDAA'12), that exemption extends to financial entities engaged in transactions with NIOC and NITC (Sec. 104(c)(4)(C)). Most of CISADA, including sanctions under this section, ceases to be effective when President removes Iran's designation as a sponsor of acts of international terrorism and that country has ceased its pursuit of WMD (Sec. 401; 22 U.S.C. 8551).
Sec. 104A (22 U.S.C. 8513A)	Anti-money laundering Anti-terrorism (financing) Nonproliferation	Expands restriction established in Sec. 104 (above) to also apply to any foreign financial institution that facilitates, participates, or assists in activities identified in Sec. 104(c).	Requires Secretary of the Treasury to issue new regulations	Secretary of the Treasury may waive if he finds it "necessary to the national interest" to do so (subsec. (f)). Most of CISADA, including sanctions under this section, ceases to be effective when President removes Iran's designation as a sponsor of acts of international terrorism and that country has ceased its pursuit of WMD (Sec. 401; 22 U.S.C. 8551).
Sec. 105 (22 U.S.C. 8514)	Human rights	Imposes sanctions on individuals the President identifies as responsible for or complicit in the human rights crackdown around the 2009 national election. Sanctions include visa ineligibility and IEEPA-related economic restrictions.	Statutory requirement of the President	President may terminate sanctions when he determines and certifies that the government of Iran has released political prisoners detained around the June 2009 election; ceased related objectionable activities; investigated related killings, arrests, and abuses; and made public commitment to establishing an independent judiciary and upholding international human rights standards. Most of CISADA, including sanctions under

Statutory Basis	Rationale	Restriction	Authority To Impose	Authority To Lift or Waive
				this section, ceases to be effective when President removes Iran's designation as a sponsor of acts of international terrorism and that country has ceased its pursuit of WMD (Sec. 401; 22 U.S.C. 8551).
				President may waive if he finds it "in the national interest" to do so (Sec. 401(b)).
Sec. 105A (22 U.S.C. 8514A)	Human rights	Imposes sanctions on any individual the President identifies as providing goods or technology to the government of Iran to facilitate human rights abuses, including "sensitive technology." Includes making such materials available to the IRGC. Sanctions include visa ineligibility and IEEPA-related economic restrictions.	Statutory requirement of the President	President may terminate sanctions when he determines an individual has taken steps toward stopping objectionable activity, and will not reengage. Most of CISADA, including sanctions under this section, ceases to be effective when President removes Iran's designation as a sponsor of acts of international terrorism and that country has ceased its pursuit of WMD (Sec. 401; 22 U.S.C. 8551). President may waive if he finds it "in the national interest" to do so (Sec. 401(b)).
Sec. 105B (22 U.S.C. 8514B)	Human rights (freedom of expression and assembly)	Imposes sanctions on any individual the President identifies as engaging in censorship or limiting the freedom of assembly. Sanctions include visa ineligibility and IEEPA-related economic restrictions.	Statutory requirement of the President	Most of CISADA, including sanctions under this section, ceases to be effective when President removes Iran's designation as a sponsor of acts of international terrorism and that country has ceased its pursuit of WMD (Sec. 401; 22 U.S.C. 8551). President may waive if he finds it "in the national interest" to do so (Sec. 401(b)).
Sec. 105C (22 U.S.C. 8514C)	Human rights (diversion of food and medicine)	Imposes sanctions on any individual the President identifies as diverting food and medicine from reaching the Iranian people. Sanctions include visa ineligibility and IEEPA-related economic restrictions.	Statutory requirement of the President	Most of CISADA, including sanctions under this section, ceases to be effective when President removes Iran's designation as a sponsor of acts of international terrorism and that country has ceased its pursuit of WMD (Sec. 401; 22 U.S.C. 8551). President may waive if he finds it "in the

Statutory Basis	Rationale	Restriction	Authority To Impose	Authority To Lift or Waive
				national interest" to do so (Sec. 401(b)).
Sec. 106 (22 U.S.C. 8515)	Human rights (freedom of expression and assembly)	Prohibits entering into procurement contracts with any individual the President identifies as exporting sensitive technology to Iran. Sec. 412, Iran Threat Reduction and Syria Human Rights Act (ITRSHRA), further defines "sensitive technology."	Statutory requirement of the President	President may exempt some products defined in specific trade laws and IEEPA. Most of CISADA, including sanctions under this section, ceases to be effective when President removes Iran's designation as a sponsor of acts of international terrorism and that country has ceased its pursuit of WMD (Sec. 401; 22 U.S.C. 8551). President may waive if he finds it "in the national interest" to do so (Sec. 401(b)).
Sec. 108 (22 U.S.C. 8516)	International obligations	President may issue any regulations to comply with U.N. Security Council resolutions.	Discretion of the President	Discretion of the President. Most of CISADA, including sanctions under this section, ceases to be effective when President removes Iran's designation as a sponsor of acts of international terrorism and that country has ceased its pursuit of WMD (Sec. 401; 22 U.S.C. 8551).
Sec. 303 (22 U.S.C. 8543)	Export controls (nonproliferation; anti-terrorism)	President may identify and designate a country as a "Destination of Division Concern" if he finds it diverts export-controlled goods and technology to Iran that would materially contribute to that state's development of WMD, delivery systems, and international terrorism. President may delay or deny export licenses.	Discretion of the President	President terminates designation—and ensuing trade restrictions—on determining that country "has adequately strengthened the export control system." Most of CISADA, including sanctions under this section, ceases to be effective when President removes Iran's designation as a sponsor of acts of international terrorism and that country has ceased its pursuit of WMD (Sec. 401; 22 U.S.C. 8551).

NATIONAL DEFENSE AUTHORIZATION ACT FOR FISCAL YEAR 2012 (NDAA 2012)

(Sec. 1245 of P.L. 112-81; 22 U.S.C. 8513a; as amended)

Statutory Basis	Rationale	Restriction	Authority To Impose	Authority To Lift or Waive
Sec. 1245	Anti-money laundering	Designates Iran's financial sector, including its Central Bank, as a "primary money laundering concern."	Statutory requirement	President may delay imposition of sanctions if government of primary jurisdiction reduces its crude oil purchases from Iran. Renewable

Statutory Basis	Rationale	Restriction	Authority To Impose	Authority To Lift or Waive
		—Requires the President to block and prohibit all transactions of any Iranian financial institution under U.S. jurisdiction.		every 180 days.
		—Requires the President to prohibit opening of correspondent and payable-through accounts for any institution that conducts transactions for the Central Bank of Iran.		President may waive imposition if he finds it "in the national security interest of the United States" to do so.
		—Authorizes the President to impose IEEPA-based sanctions.		

IRAN THREAT REDUCTION AND SYRIA HUMAN RIGHTS ACT OF 2012 (ITRSHRA)

(P.L. 112-158; 22 U.S.C. 8701 et seq.)

Statutory Basis	Rationale	Restriction	Authority To Impose	Authority To Lift or Waive
Sec. 211 (22 U.S.C. 8721)	Nonproliferation Anti-terrorism	President imposes IEEPA-based sanctions on any person he determines has engaged in transactions relating to providing a vessel or insuring a shipping service that materially contributes to the government of Iran's proliferation activities.	Statutory requirement	President may waive imposition if he finds it "vital to the national security interests of the United States" to do so. Most of ITR, including sanctions under this section, ceases to be effective when President removes Iran's designation as a sponsor of acts of international terrorism and that country has ceased its pursuit of WMD (Sec. 401, CISADA; 22 U.S.C. 8551) (Sec. 605; 22 U.S.C. 8785).
Sec. 212 (22 U.S.C. 8722)	Nonproliferation Anti-terrorism	President imposes IEEPA- and Iran Sanctions Act- (ISA) based sanctions (see above) on any person he determines has provided underwriting services or insurance for NIOC or NITC.	Statutory requirement	President may terminate if objectionable activity has ceased. Most of ITR, including sanctions under this section, ceases to be effective when President removes Iran's designation as a sponsor of acts of international terrorism and that country has ceased its pursuit of WMD (Sec. 401, CISADA; 22 U.S.C. 8551) (Sec. 605; 22 U.S.C. 8785).
Sec. 213 (22 U.S.C. 8723)	Nonproliferation Anti-terrorism	President imposes IEEPA- and ISA-based sanctions (see above) on any person he determines has engaged in transactions relating	Statutory requirement	Most of ITR, including sanctions under this section, ceases to be effective when President removes Iran's designation as a sponsor of

Statutory Basis	Rationale	Restriction	Authority To Impose	Authority To Lift or Waive
		to Iran's sovereign debt.		acts of international terrorism and that country has ceased its pursuit of WMD (Sec. 401, CISADA; 22 U.S.C. 8551) (Sec. 605; 22 U.S.C. 8785).
Sec. 217 (22 U.S.C. 8724)	Nonproliferation Anti-terrorism	Requires President to certify that the Central Bank of Iran is not engaging in activities related to WMD or terrorism before he lifts IEEPA-based sanctions imposed pursuant to E.O. 13599 (see **Table 2**). Requires President to certify that sanctions evaders are engaged in activities related to WMD or terrorism before he lifts IEEPA-based sanctions imposed pursuant to E.O. 13608 (see **Table 2**).	Statutory requirement	President may still lift sanctions, but is slowed in doing so and must certify on new conditions relating to terrorism and proliferation.
Sec. 218 (22 U.S.C. 8725)	Nonproliferation Anti-terrorism	Extends IEEPA-based sanctions imposed on parent companies to their foreign subsidiaries, to prohibit transactions with the government of Iran.	Statutory requirement	Most of ITR, including sanctions under this section, ceases to be effective when President removes Iran's designation as a sponsor of acts of international terrorism and that country has ceased its pursuit of WMD (Sec. 401, CISADA; 22 U.S.C. 8551) (Sec. 605; 22 U.S.C. 8785).
Sec. 220(c) (22 U.S.C. 8726(c))	Nonproliferation Anti-terrorism	President may impose IEEPA-based sanctions on financial messaging services that facilitate transactions for the Central Bank of Iran or other restricted financial institutions.	At the President's discretion	President's discretion. Most of ITR, including sanctions under this section, ceases to be effective when President removes Iran's designation as a sponsor of acts of international terrorism and that country has ceased its pursuit of WMD (Sec. 401, CISADA; 22 U.S.C. 8551) (Sec. 605; 22 U.S.C. 8785).
Sec. 221 (22 U.S.C. 8727)	Nonproliferation Anti-terrorism Human rights	Requires the President to identify senior Iranian government officials involved in proliferation, support of terrorism, or human rights violations. Requires the Secretaries of State and Homeland Security to, respectively, deny identified persons and their family members	Statutory requirement	President may waive if he finds it "essential to the national interests of the United States" and notifies Congress in advance. Most of ITR, including sanctions under this section, ceases to be effective when President removes Iran's designation as a sponsor of

Statutory Basis	Rationale	Restriction	Authority To Impose	Authority To Lift or Waive
		visas and entry into the United States.		acts of international terrorism and that country has ceased its pursuit of WMD (Sec. 401, CISADA; 22 U.S.C. 8551) (Sec. 605; 22 U.S.C. 8785).
Sec. 301 (22 U.S.C. 8741)	National security Nonproliferation	Requires the President to identify members, agents, and affiliates of the IRGC and impose IEEPA-based sanctions. Requires the Secretaries of State and Homeland Security to, respectively, deny identified persons and their family members visas and entry into the United States.	Statutory requirement	President may waive if he finds it "vital to the national security interests of the United States to do so." Most of ITR, including sanctions under this section, ceases to be effective when President removes Iran's designation as a sponsor of acts of international terrorism and that country has ceased its pursuit of WMD (Sec. 401, CISADA; 22 U.S.C. 8551) (Sec. 605; 22 U.S.C. 8785).
Sec. 302 (22 U.S.C. 8742)	National security Nonproliferation	Requires the President to identify those who materially engage in support or transactions with the IRGC or related entities subject to IEEPA-based sanctions. Further requires the President to impose ISA-based sanctions on and additional IEEPA-based sanctions on those he identifies. President is not required to publicly identify such individual if "doing so would cause damage to the national security of the United States."	Statutory requirement	President may terminate when he determines objectionable activities have ceased. President may waive if activities have ceased or if "it is essential to the national security interests of the United States to do so." President may forego imposing sanctions if similar exception has been made under Sec. 104(c) of CISADA (see above). Most of ITR, including sanctions under this section, ceases to be effective when President removes Iran's designation as a sponsor of acts of international terrorism and that country has ceased its pursuit of WMD (Sec. 401, CISADA; 22 U.S.C. 8551) (Sec. 605; 22 U.S.C. 8785).
Sec. 303 (22 U.S.C. 8743)	Nonproliferation United Nations compliance	President is required to identify any agency of a foreign country that materially assists or engages in transactions with IRGC or any entity subject to U.N. Security Council sanctions. President may cut off most foreign aid, deny	Statutory requirement; however, President selects specific actions	President may terminate if objectionable activities have ceased, or if "it is essential to the national security interests of the United States to terminate such measures." President may waive imposition of any

Statutory Basis	Rationale	Restriction	Authority To Impose	Authority To Lift or Waive
		arms sales and transfers, deny export licenses, require opposition to loans to that foreign country in the international financial institutions, deny USG financial assistance, or impose other IEEPA-based sanctions.		measure if he explains his decision to Congress (and justification may be subsequent to action taken). Most of ITR, including sanctions under this section, ceases to be effective when President removes Iran's designation as a sponsor of acts of international terrorism and that country has ceased its pursuit of WMD (Sec. 401, CISADA; 22 U.S.C. 8551) (Sec. 605; 22 U.S.C. 8785).
Sec. 411 (22 U.S.C. 8751)	Human rights Nonproliferation Anti-terrorism	Requires the President to maintain IEEPA-based sanctions pursuant to E.O. 13606 (see **Table 2**) until he certifies Iran has ceased its support of international terrorism and pursuit of weapons proliferation, under Sec. 401, CISADA (see above).	Statutory requirement	President's determination.
Sec. 501 (22 U.S.C. 8771)	Nonproliferation	Requires the Secretaries of State and Homeland Security to, respectively, deny visas and entry into the United States to Iranian citizens who seek education in the United States related to energy, nuclear science, or nuclear engineering.	Statutory requirement	Most of ITR, including sanctions under this section, ceases to be effective when President removes Iran's designation as a sponsor of acts of international terrorism and that country has ceased its pursuit of WMD (Sec. 401, CISADA; 22 U.S.C. 8551) (Sec. 605; 22 U.S.C. 8785).

IRAN FREEDOM AND COUNTER-PROLIFERATION ACT OF 2012

(Title XII, subtitle D, of National Defense Authorization Act for Fiscal Year 2013; **NDAA 2013**; P.L. 112-239; 22 U.S.C. 8801 et seq.)

Statutory Basis	Rationale	Restriction	Authority To Impose	Authority To Lift or Waive
Sec. 1244 (22 U.S.C. 8803)	Nonproliferation	Designates entities that operate Iran's ports, and entities in energy, shipping, and shipbuilding, including NITC, IRISL, and NIOC, and their affiliates, as "entities of proliferation concern." Requires the President to block transactions and interests in property under U.S. jurisdiction of such entities. Requires the President to impose ISA-based sanctions on any person who knowingly engages	Statutory requirement	Humanitarian-related transactions are exempted. President may exempt transactions related to Afghanistan reconstruction and development, if he determines it in the national interest to do so. President may exempt application to those countries exempted from NDAA'12 requirements (see above).

Statutory Basis	Rationale	Restriction	Authority To Impose	Authority To Lift or Waive
		in trade related to energy, shipping, or shipbuilding sectors of Iran.		Some aspects of trade in natural gas are exempted. President may waive for 180 days if he finds it "vital to the national security of the United States" to do so.
Sec. 1245 (22 U.S.C. 8804)	Nonproliferation	Requires the President to impose ISA-based sanctions on any person who knowingly engages in trade related to precious metal, or material used in energy, shipping, or shipbuilding, if controlled by IRGC or other sanctioned entity.	Statutory requirement	President may exempt those he determines are exercising "due diligence" to comply with restrictions. President may waive for 180 days, and may renew that waiver in 6-month increments, if he finds it "vital to the national security of the United States" to do so.
Sec. 1246 (22 U.S.C. 8805)	Nonproliferation	Requires the President to impose ISA-based sanctions on any person who knowingly provides underwriting or insurance services to any sanctioned entity with respect to Iran.	Statutory requirement	Humanitarian-related transactions are exempted. President may exempt those he determines are exercising "due diligence" to comply with restrictions. President may waive for 180 days, and may renew that waiver in 6-month increments, if he finds it "vital to the national security of the United States" to do so.
Sec. 1247 (22 U.S.C. 8806)	Nonproliferation	Requires the President to prohibit any correspondent or payable-through account by a foreign financial institution that is found to facilitate a "significant financial transaction" on behalf of any Iranian Specially Designated National (SDN).	Statutory requirement	Humanitarian-related transactions are exempted. President may exempt application to those countries exempted from NDAA'12 requirements (see above). President may waive for 180 days, and may renew that waiver in 6-month increments, if he finds it "vital to the national security of the United States" to do so.
Sec. 1248 (22 U.S.C. 8807)	Human rights	Requires the President to apply Sec. 105(c), CISADA-based sanctions (see above) to the Islamic Republic of Iran Broadcasting and the	Statutory requirement	President may waive if he finds it "in the national interest" to do so (Sec. 401(b),

Statutory Basis	Rationale	Restriction	Authority To Impose	Authority To Lift or Waive
		President of that entity, and to add this entity and individual to the SDN list.		CISADA). President may terminate sanctions when he determines and certifies that the government of Iran has released political prisoners detained around the June 2009 election; ceased related objectionable activities; investigated related killings, arrests, and abuses; and made public commitment to establishing an independent judiciary and upholding international human rights standards (Sec. 105(d), CISADA).

Notes: AECA = Arms Export Control Act; CISADA = Comprehensive Iran Sanctions, Accountability, and Divestment Act of 2010; DNI = Director of National Intelligence; E.O. = Executive Order; FTO = Foreign Terrorist Organization; IAEA = International Atomic Energy Agency; IEEPA = International Emergency Economic Powers Act; IFI = International Financial Institution; IFSA = Iran Freedom Support Act; IIANA = Iran-Iraq Arms Non-Proliferation Act of 1992; INA = Immigration and Nationality Act of 1952; INKSA = Iran, North Korea, Syria Nonproliferation Act; IRGC = Iranian Revolutionary Guard Corps; ISA = Iran Sanctions Act of 1996; ITRSHRA = Iran Threat Reduction and Syria Human Rights Act of 2012; NDAA = National Defense Authorization Act; NEA = National Emergencies Act; NICO = Naftiran Intertrade Company; NIOC = National Iranian Oil Company; NITC = National Iranian Tanker Company; SDN = Specially Designated National; TSRA = Trade Sanctions Reform Act of 2000; UNICEF = U.N. Children's Fund; UNPA = United Nations Participation Act of 1945; UNSC = United Nations Security Council; USC = United States Code; USML = United States Munitions List; USTR = U.S. Trade Representative; WMD = Weapons of Mass Destruction.

Table 2. Executive Orders Issued to Meet Statutory Requirements To Impose Economic Sanctions on Iran

Executive Order	Underlying Statute	Restriction	Authority To Lift or Waive
E.O. 12170 (November 14, 1979)	IEEPA / NEA	*Declares a national emergency exists relating to 1979 events in Iran;* blocks Iranian government property subject to U.S. jurisdiction. Secretary of the Treasury administers.	President
E.O. 12938 (November 14, 1994)	IEEPA / NEA AECA (also invoked in Sec. 3(b)(1), INKSA)	*Declares a national emergency exists relating to the proliferation of weapons of mass destruction and the means of delivery.* Succeeds and replaces similar authorities of 1990 and 1994. Establishes export controls, sanctions affecting foreign aid, procurement, imports, on proliferators. Establishes sanctions—affecting foreign aid, IFI support, credits, arms sales, exports, imports, landing rights—targeting foreign countries that produce or use chemical or biological weapons. Secretaries of State, Commerce, Defense, and the Treasury administer.	President
E.O. 12957 (March 15, 1995)	IEEPA / NEA	*Declares a national emergency exists relating to Iran's proliferation activities;* prohibits persons under U.S. jurisdiction from entering into certain transactions with respect to Iranian petroleum resources. Secretaries of the Treasury and State administer.	President Sec. 101(a), IFSA, codifies this EO. The President must notify Congress 15 days in advance of its termination, unless exigent circumstances justify acting first.
E.O. 12959 (May 6, 1995)	IEEPA / NEA ISDC '85	Expands national emergency set forth in E.O. 12957; prohibits entering into new investment. Secretaries of the Treasury and State administer.	President Sec. 101(a), IFSA, codifies this EO. The President must notify Congress 15 days in advance of its termination, unless exigent circumstances justify acting first.
E.O. 13059 (August 19, 1997)	IEEPA / NEA ISDC '85	Clarifies steps taken in E.O. 12957 and E.O. 12959; prohibits most imports from Iran, exports to Iran, new investment, transactions relating to Iran-origin goods regardless of their location Secretaries of the Treasury and State administer.	President Sec. 101(a), IFSA, codifies this EO. The President must notify Congress 15 days in advance of its termination, unless exigent circumstances justify acting first.

Executive Order	Underlying Statute	Restriction	Authority To Lift or Waive
E.O. 13224 (September 23, 2001)	IEEPA / NEA UNPA'45 (also invoked in Sec. 211, ITRSHRA)	*Declares a national emergency exists relating to international terrorism*, in the aftermath of events of September 11, 2001; blocks property and prohibits transactions with persons who commit, threaten to commit, or support terrorism. Generates a list of designated individuals who are incorporated into the Specially Designated Nationals (SDN) list.	President
		Secretaries of the Treasury, State, Homeland Security, and the Attorney General administer.	
E.O. 13382 (June 28, 2005)	IEEPA / NEA (also invoked in Sec. 211, ITRSHRA)	Expands national emergency set forth in E.O. 12938; blocks property of WMD proliferators and their supporters.	President
		Secretaries of State, the Treasury, and the Attorney General administer.	
E.O. 13438 (July 17, 2007)	IEEPA / NEA	Expands national emergency relating to events in Iraq and set forth in E.O. 13303, May 22, 2003; blocks property of certain persons who threaten stabilization efforts in Iraq.	President
		Secretaries of the Treasury, State, and Defense administer.	
E.O. 13553 (September 28, 2010)	IEEPA / NEA CISADA	Expands national emergency set forth in E.O. 12957; blocks property of certain persons with respect to human rights abuses by the government of Iran. Generates a list of designated individuals for whom property under U.S. jurisdiction is blocked. Imposes sanctions on those who enter into transactions with designated individuals.	President
		This is the initial implementation of requirements under CISADA.	
		Secretaries of the Treasury and State administer.	
E.O. 13574 (May 23, 2011)	IEEPA / NEA ISA '96 CISADA	Expands national emergency set forth in E.O. 12957; implements new sanctions added to ISA. Prohibits U.S. financial institutions from making loans or credits, or engaging in foreign exchange transactions. Prohibits imports from, and blocks property of, a sanctioned person.	President
		The President, and Secretaries of the Treasury and State, administer.	

Executive Order	Underlying Statute	Restriction	Authority To Lift or Waive
E.O. 13590 (November 20, 2011)	IEEPA / NEA	Expands national emergency set forth in E.O. 12957; blocks property of those who trade in goods, services, technology, or support for Iran's energy and petrochemical sectors. Prohibits Ex-Im Bank from entering into transactions with sanctioned person. Requires Federal Reserve to deny goods and services. Prohibits U.S. financial institutions from making most loans or credits. Secretaries of State, the Treasury, and Commerce, the U.S. Trade Representative (USTR), Chairman of Federal Reserve Board, and President of Ex-Im Bank, administer.	President
E.O. 13599 (February 5, 2012)	IEEPA / NEA NDAA '12	Expands national emergency set forth in E.O. 12957; blocks property of the government of Iran and Iranian financial institutions, including the Central Bank of Iran. Secretaries of the Treasury, State, and Energy, and DNI administer.	President Sec. 217, ITRSHRA, requires the President notify Congress 90 days in advance of termination of this E.O., and certify a number of objectionable activities have ceased.
E.O. 13606 (April 22, 2012)	IEEPA / NEA	Expands, in the case of Iran, national emergency set forth in E.O. 12957; blocks the property and suspends entry into the United States of persons found to commit human rights abuses by the governments of Iran and Syria, facilitated misuse of information technology. Generates new list of SDN. Secretaries of the Treasury and State administer.	President Sec. 411, ITRSHRA, requires the President notify Congress 30 days in advance of termination of this E.O., and certify a number of objectionable activities have ceased pursuant to Sec. 401, CISADA.
E.O. 13608 (May 1, 2012)	IEEPA / NEA	Expands, in the case of Iran, national emergency set forth in E.O. 12957; prohibits transactions with and suspends entry into the United States of foreign sanctions evaders. Generates new list of SDN. Secretaries of the Treasury and State administer.	President Sec. 217, ITRSHRA, requires the President notify Congress 30 days in advance of termination of this E.O., and certify a number of objectionable activities have ceased pursuant to Sec. 401, CISADA.

Executive Order	Underlying Statute	Restriction	Authority To Lift or Waive
E.O. 13622 (July 30, 2012)	IEEPA / NEA NDAA '12	Expands national emergency set forth in E.O. 12957; authorizes sanctions on foreign financial institutions that finance activities with NIOC, NICO. Prohibits correspondent and payable-through accounts. Prohibits Ex-Im financing, designation as a primary dealer of U.S. debt instruments, access to U.S. financial institutions. Blocks property, denies imports and exports. The President, and Secretaries of the Treasury, State, and Commerce, the USTR, Chairman of Federal Reserve Board, and President of Ex-Im Bank, administer.	President
E.O. 13628 (October 9, 2012)	IEEPA / NEA ISA '96 CISADA ITRSHRA INA	Expands national emergency set forth in E.O. 12957; primarily implements ITRSHRA. Further prohibits U.S. financial institutions from making loans or credits, foreign exchange transactions, and transfers or credits between financial institutions. Blocks property of those who deal in equity or debt instruments of a sanctioned person. Prohibits imports, exports. Extends sanctions to other officers of sanctioned entities. Blocks property affiliated with human rights abusers, including those who limit freedom of expression. Denies access to certain financing tools, property, and imports, if one engaged in expansion of Iran's refined petroleum sector. Blocks entry into the United States of those who engage in certain human rights abuses. The President, and Secretaries of the Treasury, State, and Commerce, the USTR, Chairman of Federal Reserve Board, and President of Ex-Im Bank, administer.	President

CRS-26

Executive Order	Underlying Statute	Restriction	Authority To Lift or Waive
E.O. 13645 (June 3, 2013)	IEEPA / NEA CISADA IFCA INA	Expands national emergency set forth in E.O. 12957; imposes restrictions on foreign financial institutions engaged in transactions relating to, or maintaining accounts dominated by, Iran's currency (*rial*). Prohibits opening or maintaining U.S.-based payable-through correspondent accounts. Blocks property under U.S. jurisdiction. Imposes restrictions on those, including foreign financial institutions, found to be materially assisting in any way an Iran-related SDN. Imposes restrictions on those found to engage in transactions related to Iran's petroleum or related products. Requires the Secretary of State to impose restrictions on financing (Federal Reserve, Ex-Im Bank, commercial banks) on those found to engage in significant transactions related to Iran's automotive sector. Blocks property of those found to have engage in diversion of goods and services intended for the people of Iran The President, and Secretaries of the Treasury, State, Homeland Security, and Commerce, the USTR, Chairman of Federal Reserve Board, and President of Ex-Im Bank, administer.	President

Notes: AECA = Arms Export Control Act; CISADA = Comprehensive Iran Sanctions, Accountability, and Divestment Act of 2010; DNI = Director of National Intelligence; E.O. = Executive Order; IEEPA = International Emergency Economic Powers Act; IFI = International Financial Institution; IFCA = Iran Freedom and Counter-proliferation Act of 2012; IFSA = Iran Freedom Support Act; INA = Immigration and Nationality Act of 1952; INKSA = Iran, North Korea, Syria Nonproliferation Act; ISA = Iran Sanctions Act of 1996; ITRSHRA = Iran Threat Reduction and Syria Human Rights Act of 2012; NDAA = National Defense Authorization Act; NEA = National Emergencies Act; NICO = Naftiran Intertrade Company; NIOC = National Iranian Oil Company; SDN = Specially Designated National; UNPA = United Nations Participation Act of 1945; USTR = U.S. Trade Representative.

Author Contact Information

Dianne E. Rennack
Specialist in Foreign Policy Legislation
drennack@crs.loc.gov, 7-7608

www.ingramcontent.com/pod-product-compliance
Lightning Source LLC
Chambersburg PA
CBHW052025280526
45793CB00005B/1134